Theory Book 1 · Elementary

Theory

Willard A. Palmer · Morton Manus · Amanda Vick Lethco

Additional Pages: Andrew Higgins
Additional Artwork/Engraving: Oliver Wood
Additional Proofing: Leonie McCaughren
Cover Design: Holly Fraser

Produced by
Alfred Publishing Co. (UK) Ltd.
Burnt Mill, Elizabeth Way,
Harlow
Essex, CM20 2HX

alfreduk.com

ISBN-10: 1-4706-1309-3
ISBN-13: 978-1-4706-1309-9

Cover and Interior Illustrations by David Silverman (Painted by Cheryl Hennigar)

Alfred's

Basic Graded Piano Course

Theory Book

Elementary

This Alfred's Basic Graded Piano Course Theory Book was written in response to many requests from teachers for an Alfred Course that enables students to pass the graded exams that are so much a part of the learning experience throughout the world. It uses the Lesson Book to introduce sight-reading and technique, as well as preparation for pieces, alongside this correlated Theory Book to prepare for the Theory exam.

By including examples from previous papers and a mock theory paper that the student might expect to see in the exam, you, as a teacher can judge perfectly the appropriate time to enter your pupil for the graded exam. This will make passing a formality and, more importantly, give your pupil the confidence to achieve the merits and distinctions that inspire and reward their hard work.

Assign with Lesson Book p.4

The Keyboard

The keyboard is made up of white keys and black keys.
The black keys are in groups of 2's and 3's.

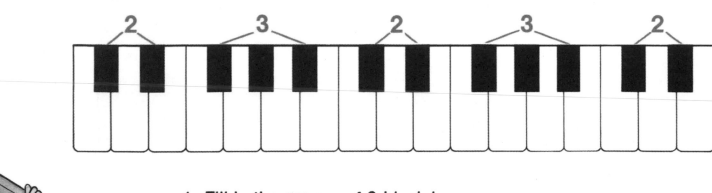

1. Fill in the groups of 2 black keys.

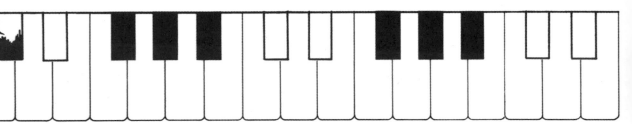

2. Fill in the groups of 3 black keys.

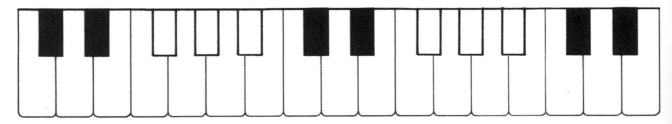

3. Draw a circle around each group of 2 black keys.

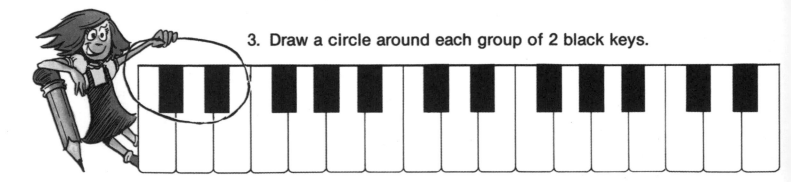

4. Draw a circle around each group of 3 black keys.

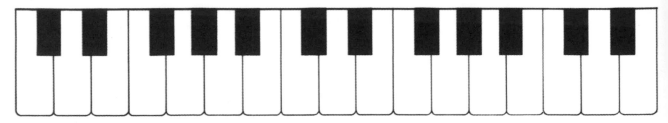

Time to Count!

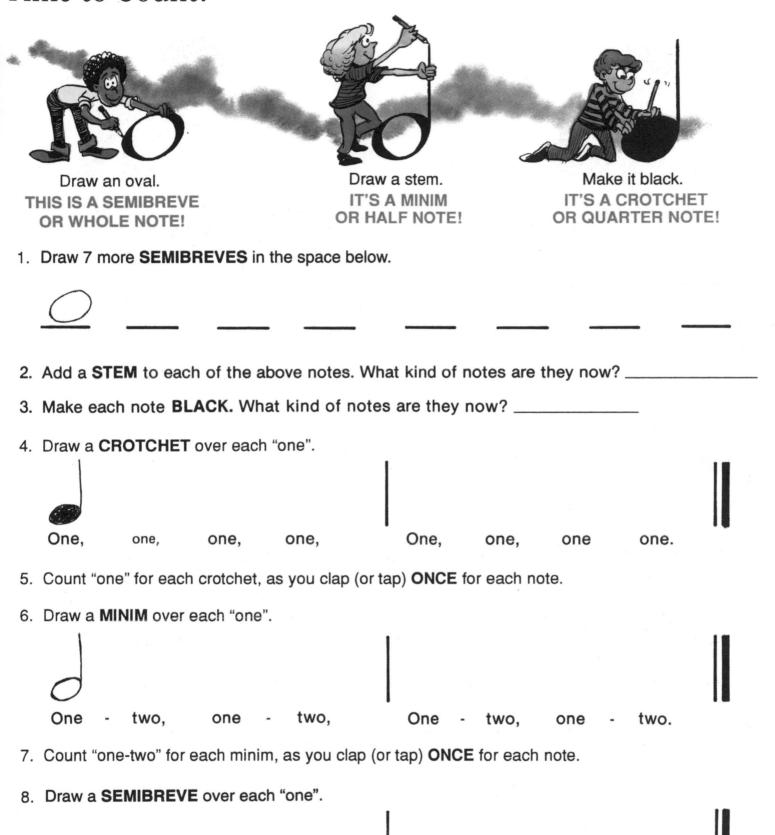

Draw an oval.
**THIS IS A SEMIBREVE
OR WHOLE NOTE!**

Draw a stem.
**IT'S A MINIM
OR HALF NOTE!**

Make it black.
**IT'S A CROTCHET
OR QUARTER NOTE!**

1. Draw 7 more **SEMIBREVES** in the space below.

2. Add a **STEM** to each of the above notes. What kind of notes are they now? _____

3. Make each note **BLACK.** What kind of notes are they now? _____

4. Draw a **CROTCHET** over each "one".

One,   one,   one,   one,   One,   one,   one   one.

5. Count "one" for each crotchet, as you clap (or tap) **ONCE** for each note.

6. Draw a **MINIM** over each "one".

One - two,   one - two,   One - two,   one - two.

7. Count "one-two" for each minim, as you clap (or tap) **ONCE** for each note.

8. Draw a **SEMIBREVE** over each "one".

One - two - three - four,   One - two - three - four.

9. Count "one-two-three-four" for each semibreve, as you clap (or tap) **ONCE** for each note.

Note to Teachers: All rhythm exercises in this book are based on time signatures in which a crotchet gets one count.

Note-Stems and Bar Lines

Note-stems that point **up**
are on the **RIGHT** side
of the note-head!

Note-stems that point **down**
are on the **LEFT** side
of the note-head!

1. Add note-stems POINTING UP.

2. Add note-stems POINTING DOWN.

3. Draw a **BAR LINE** | dividing each of the above examples into **2 EQUAL BARS**
   (4 notes in each bar).

4. Draw a **DOUBLE BAR** ‖ after the last note of each of the above examples.
   Notice that the double bar has one THIN line and one THICK line. It is used at the END.

5. Play EXAMPLE 1. Use R.H. 3 on any key you choose. Count aloud as you play.

6. Play EXAMPLE 2. Use L.H. 3 on any key you choose. Count aloud as you play.

How Many Counts?

7. In the square below each note, write the number of counts the note receives.

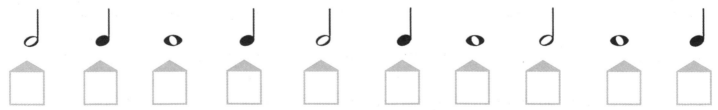

Name That Key!

The **MUSICAL ALPHABET** has 7 letters: A   B   C   D   E   F   G

1. Write the MUSICAL ALPHABET in the squares on this keyboard. Begin with **A**.

A is between the
2nd & 3rd keys
of any
3 black-key group!

2. Find all the **A**'s on this keyboard. Print an **A** on each one.

B is on the RIGHT
of any
3 black-key group!

3. Find all the **B**'s on this keyboard. Print a **B** on each one.

Assign with Lesson Book p.1

C is on the LEFT
of any
2 black-key group!

4. Find all the **C**'s on this keyboard. Print a **C** on each one.

D is in the MIDDLE
of any
2 black-key group!

5. Find all the **D**'s on this keyboard. Print a **D** on each one.

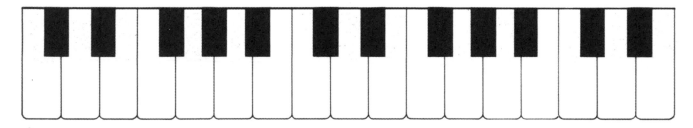

E is on the RIGHT
of any
2 black-key group!

6. Find all the **E**'s on this keyboard. Print an **E** on each one.

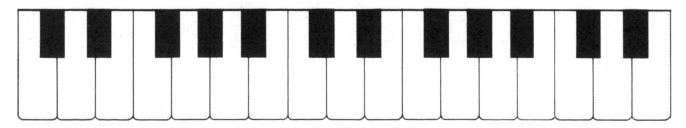

Assign with Lesson Book p.14

F is on the LEFT
of any
3 black-key group!

7. Find all the **F**'s on this keyboard. Print an **F** on each one.

G is between the
1st & 2nd keys
of any
3 black-key group!

8. Find all the **G**'s on this keyboard. Print a **G** on each one.

9. On the keyboard below, print the names of the keys in this order:

1. All the C's.   4. All the F's.   6. All the A's.
2. All the E's.   5. All the B's.   7. All the G's.
3. All the D's.

Check: Are all the notes in the order of the MUSICAL ALPHABET?

Assign with Lesson Book p.1

Spelling Games

Write the letter name on each key marked X.
Each keyboard will spell a familiar word!

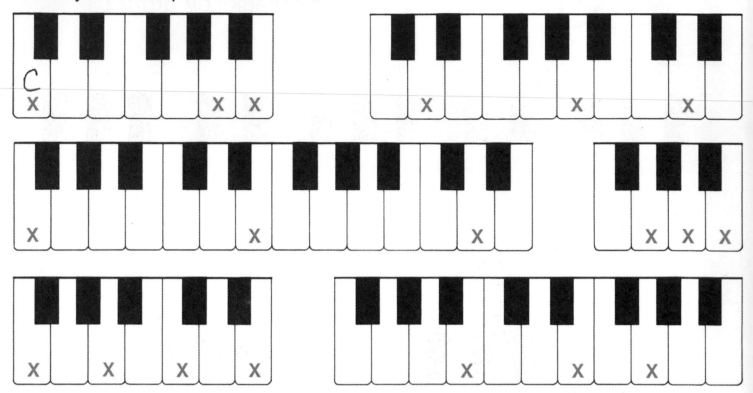

Spell BEAD on this keyboard.
Begin on the lowest B and use a higher key for each letter.

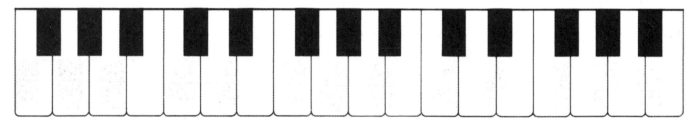

Spell ADD on this keyboard.
Begin on the lowest A and use a higher key for each letter.

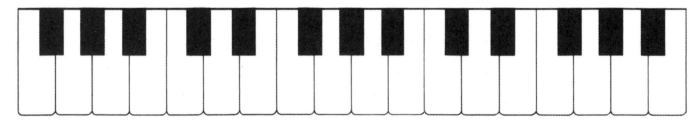

Spell CAGE on this keyboard.
Begin on the lowest C and use a higher key for each letter.

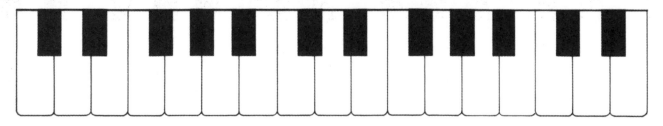

Assign with Lesson Book p.15

The Time Signature

Music has numbers at the beginning called the **TIME SIGNATURE**.
The **TOP NUMBER** tells the number of beats in each bar.
The **BOTTOM NUMBER** tells the kind of note that gets ONE beat.

$\frac{4}{4}$ means **4** beats to each bar.

$\frac{4}{4}$ a **CROTCHET** ♩ gets ONE beat.

BAR LINE   BAR LINE

← ——— BAR ——— → ← ——— BAR ——— →

$\frac{4}{4}$ One,   one,   one,   two, | One   two   three   four.

The notes in each bar must add up to **4 COUNTS!**

1. How many **CROTCHETS** can you have in each bar of $\frac{4}{4}$ time?_____
   Fill these bars with **CROTCHETS**.

   $\frac{4}{4}$

2. How many **MINIMS** can you have in each bar of $\frac{4}{4}$ time?_____
   Fill these bars with **MINIMS**.

   $\frac{4}{4}$

3. How many **SEMIBREVES** can you have in each bar of $\frac{4}{4}$ time?_____
   Fill these bars with **SEMIBREVES**.

   $\frac{4}{4}$

4. Add only **ONE NOTE** to each bar to make it complete.

   $\frac{4}{4}$

   $\frac{4}{4}$

Assign with Lesson Book p.18

A New Time Signature

3 means **3** beats to each bar.

4 a **CROTCHET** ♩ gets ONE beat.

The Dotted Minim (Half Note)

d.

COUNT 2 for the MINIM + 1 for the DOT!   COUNT: "1 - 2 - 3"

3 ♩	♩	♩	d.			d		♩	♩	♩	d
4 One,	one,	one,	One,	two	three,	One	two,	one,	One,	one,	two.

The notes in each bar must add up to **3 COUNTS!!!**

1. After the **3/4** below, draw a DOTTED MINIM over each "one".

2. Add BAR LINES.   Put a DOUBLE BAR at the end.

3
4

One-two-three, One-two-three, One-two-three, One-two-three.

3. In the square below each note, write the number of counts it receives.

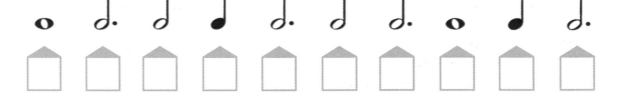

4. Under each line, write ONE NOTE equal in value to the sum of the TWO notes above it, as shown in the first example.

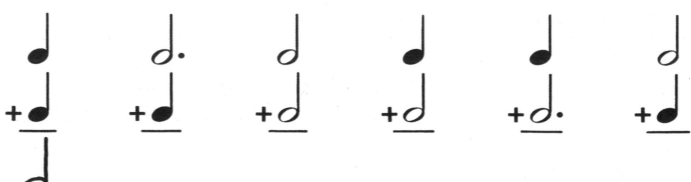

Review

Musical Matching

mf	𝅗𝅥	3/4	*p*	𝅝	*f*	♩	𝅗𝅥.

5. Draw each of the above signs in the correct squares below.
   Draw each sign TWICE; once in the LEFT column and once in the RIGHT column.

☐	piano	☐	count 4 for this note.
☐	dotted minim	☐	loud
☐	time signature	☐	count 2 for this note.
☐	crotchet	☐	means there are 3 counts in each bar.
☐	mezzo forte	☐	soft
☐	semibreve	☐	count 1 for this note.
☐	minim	☐	moderately loud
☐	forte	☐	count 3 for this note.

Assign with Lesson Book p.2

The Stave

Music is written on a **STAVE** of 5 lines and 4 spaces.

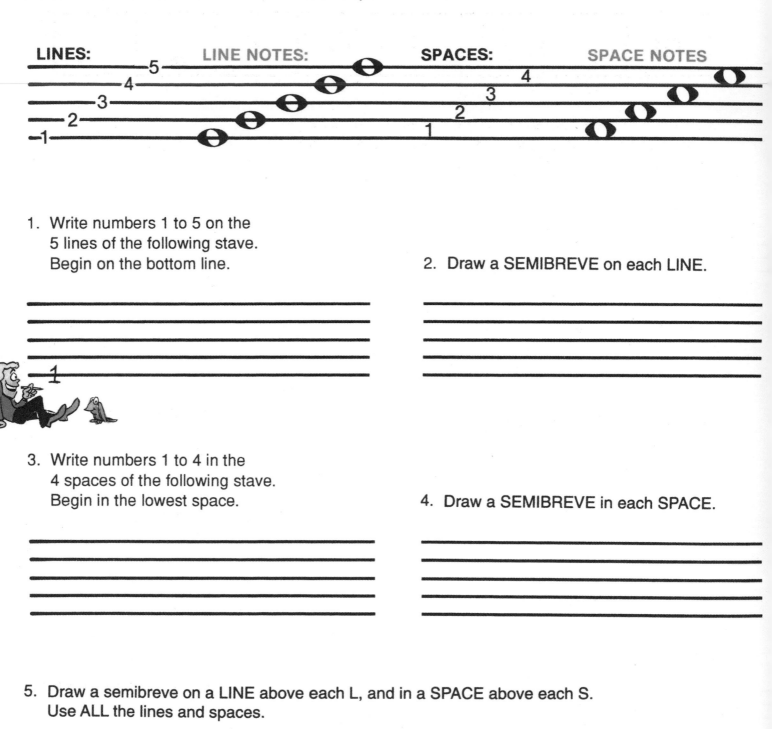

LINES: **LINE NOTES:** **SPACES:** **SPACE NOTES**

1. Write numbers 1 to 5 on the
   5 lines of the following stave.
   Begin on the bottom line.

2. Draw a SEMIBREVE on each LINE.

3. Write numbers 1 to 4 in the
   4 spaces of the following stave.
   Begin in the lowest space.

4. Draw a SEMIBREVE in each SPACE.

5. Draw a semibreve on a LINE above each L, and in a SPACE above each S.
   Use ALL the lines and spaces.

 L S S L L S L S L

More About he Stave

Stem Direction: Up or Down?

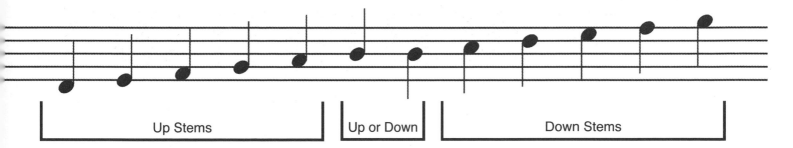

Up Stems   Up or Down   Down Stems

1. Circle the notes that are written correctly.

2. Write SEMIBREVES (whole notes) on every line.

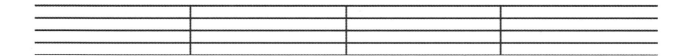

3. Write SEMIBREVES (whole notes) in each space.

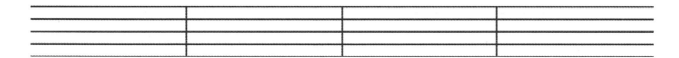

4. Add a stem to each note making sure to point it in the right direction.

13

The Bass Clef Sign

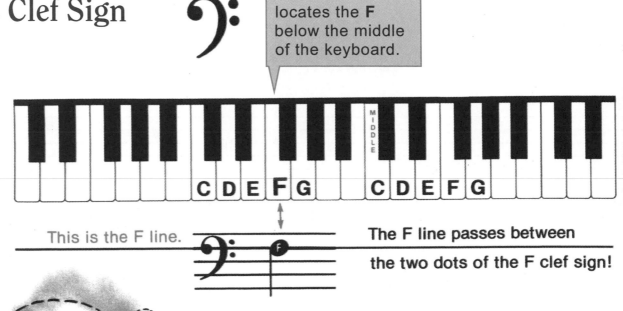

locates the **F** below the middle of the keyboard.

C D E F G   C D E F G

This is the F line.   The F line passes between the two dots of the F clef sign!

START HERE   MAKE THE TWO DOTS LAST.

1. Trace this bass clef sign:

2. Trace a whole line of BASS CLEF signs. Always begin on the F line. The two dots are in the TOP TWO SPACES.

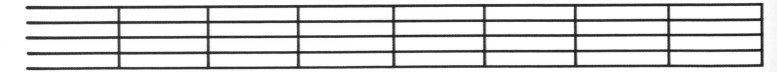

3. Draw a line of BASS CLEF signs without tracing.

4. Write the name of each note in the square below it.

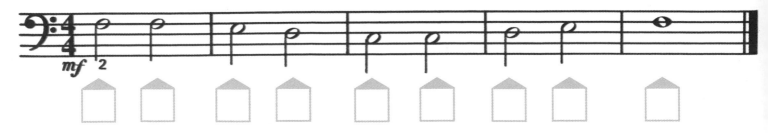

5. Play the above as you say the note names.

Assign with Lesson Book p.22

The Treble Clef Sign

locates the **G** above the middle of the keyboard.

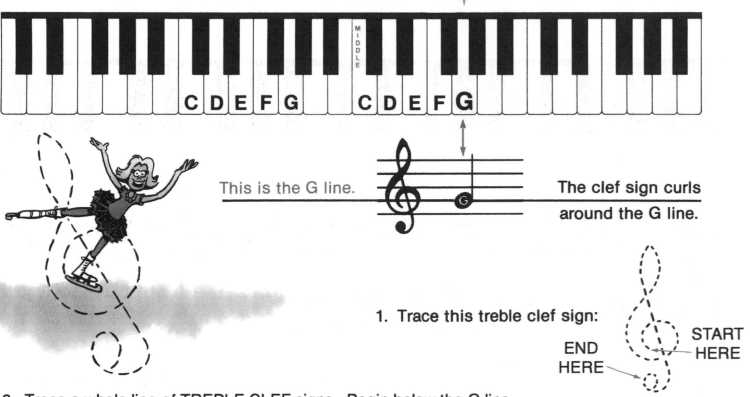

This is the G line.

The clef sign curls around the G line.

1. Trace this treble clef sign:

START HERE

END HERE

2. Trace a whole line of TREBLE CLEF signs. Begin below the G line. Curl the end of the sign below the stave.

3. Draw a line of TREBLE CLEF signs without tracing.

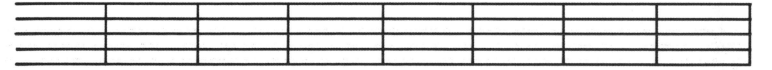

4. Write the name of each note in the square below it.

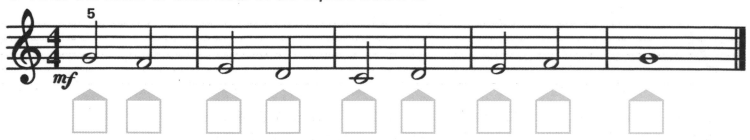

5. Play the above as you say the note names.

Assign with Lesson Book p.25

The Grand Stave

The TREBLE STAVE and the BASS STAVE combine to make the GRAND STAVE.

1. Print the letter names on this keyboard, beginning with the lowest A and ending with the highest G. You should use the complete MUSICAL ALPHABET 3 times.

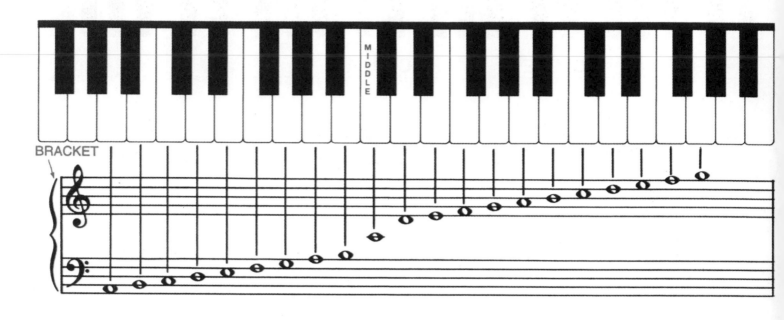

The TREBLE & BASS staves are joined together with a BRACKET and a BAR LINE to make a GRAND STAVE.

BRACKET:

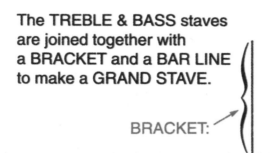

2. Trace these 3 BRACKETS.

3. Draw 3 BRACKETS without tracing.

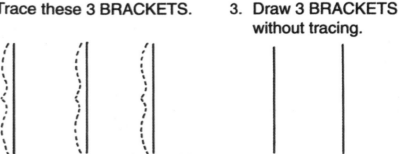

4. Join the beginning and the end of the two staves below by tracing the bar lines, then trace the BRACKET at the beginning to complete the GRAND STAVE.

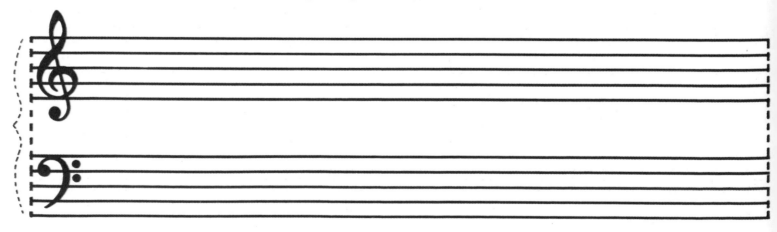

5. Write ALL the notes on the GRAND STAVE above. Use SEMIBREVES. Begin in the lowest space. Keep the notes very close together so they look the same as in the stave at the top of this page.

6. Print the name over each note.

C Position on the Grand Stave

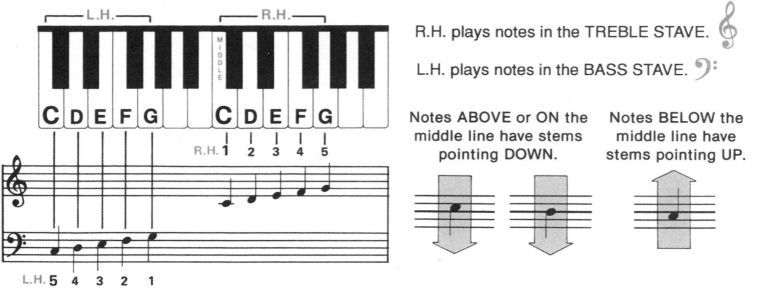

R.H. plays notes in the TREBLE STAVE.

L.H. plays notes in the BASS STAVE.

Notes ABOVE or ON the middle line have stems pointing DOWN.

Notes BELOW the middle line have stems pointing UP.

1. Write the L.H. notes in the BASS stave, under the squares. Use CROTCHETS.
   Turn the stem of the C **UP**. Turn the stems of the D E F & G **DOWN.**

2. Write the R.H. notes in the TREBLE stave, over the squares. Use CROTCHETS.
   Turn all the stems **UP.**

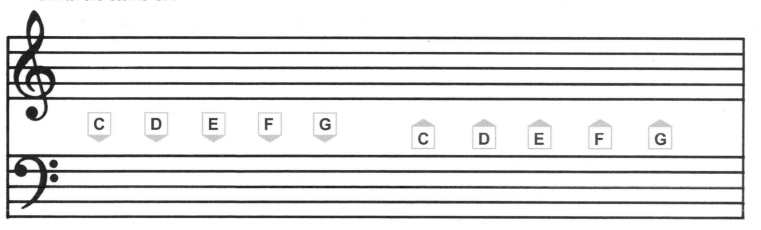

Spelling Game

3. Write the name of each note in the square below it.
   The letters in each group of squares will spell a familiar word.

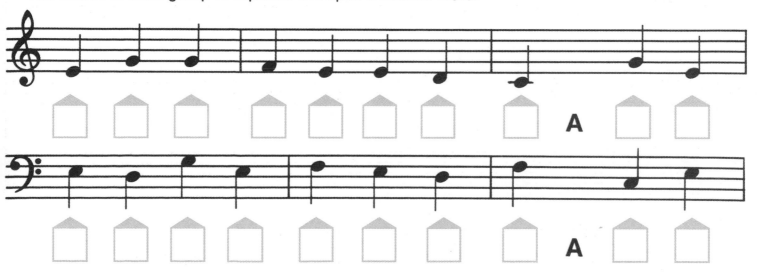

Legato Playing

LEGATO means SMOOTHLY CONNECTED.

Slurs are curved lines over or under the notes. They tell us to PLAY LEGATO.

SLUR

SLURS often divide the music into PHRASES.

A PHRASE is a musical thought or sentence. It is a fragment of melody not complete in itself. In language, it may be compared to a simple sentence, or a line of a poem.

A Sunny Day!

1. Draw a SLUR connecting the 1st note of the 1st bar to the last note of the 2nd bar.
2. Draw a SLUR connecting the 1st note of the 3rd bar to the last note of the 4th bar.
3. Draw a SLUR connecting the 1st note of the 5th bar to the last note of the 6th bar.
4. Draw a SLUR connecting the 1st note of the 7th bar to the last note of the 8th bar.

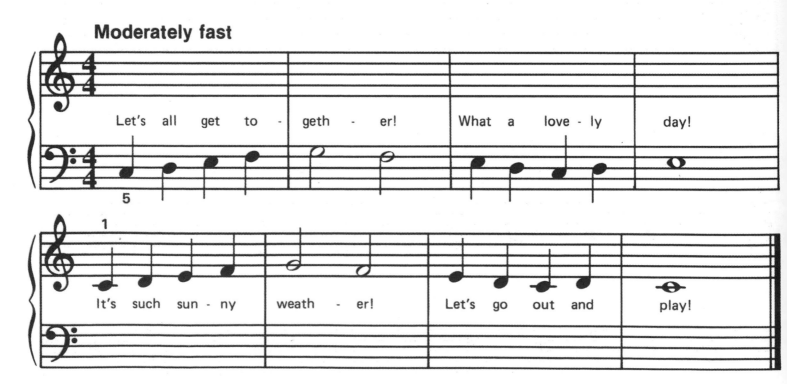

5. Over the 1st note, add a sign that means play MODERATELY LOUD.
6. Play the piece. Connect the notes of each phrase. Lift the hand at the end of each phrase.

Assign with Lesson Book p.28

Measuring 2nds

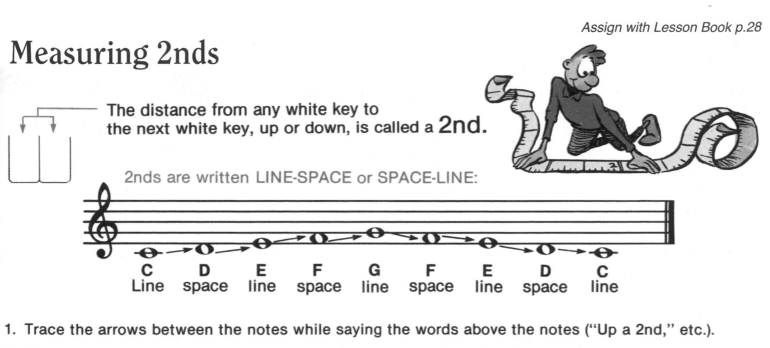

The distance from any white key to the next white key, up or down, is called a **2nd**.

2nds are written LINE-SPACE or SPACE-LINE:

C	D	E	F	G	F	E	D	C
Line	space	line	space	line	space	line	space	line

1. Trace the arrows between the notes while saying the words above the notes ("Up a 2nd," etc.).

2. Write the note name under each note, then play, saying "Up a 2nd," etc.

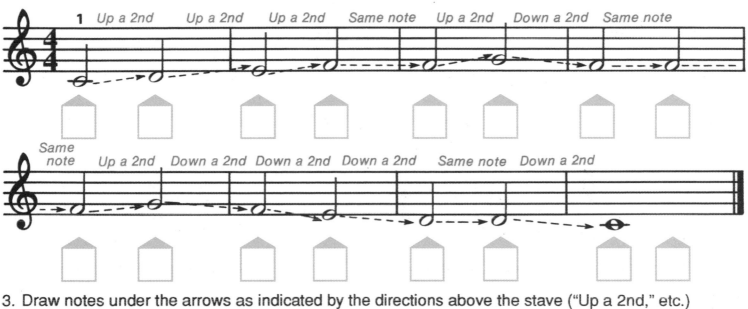

3. Draw notes under the arrows as indicated by the directions above the stave ("Up a 2nd," etc.)
   Use MINIMS for each note except the last in bar 8.
   Use a SEMIBREVE for the last note.

4. Write the note name under each note, then play, saying "Up a 2nd," etc.

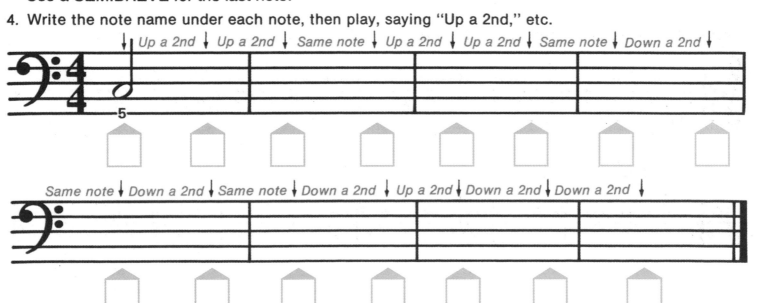

Assign with Lesson Book p.29

Tied Notes

When notes on the SAME LINE are joined by a curved line,
we call them TIED NOTES.

The key is held down for the COMBINED VALUES OF BOTH NOTES.

COUNT: "1 - 2 - 3 - 4,   1 - 2 - 3 - 4"   TOTAL, 8 counts.

1. How long would you hold the key down for each pair of tied notes?
   Write the TOTAL number of counts for each pair of tied notes in the blank spaces.

_____COUNTS.

_____COUNTS.

_____COUNTS.

_____COUNTS.

_____COUNTS.

_____COUNTS.

If the notes
are the **SAME**—
it's a **TIE**!

If the notes
are **DIFFERENT**—
it's a **SLUR**.

Hold the notes, without repeating!

Connect the notes, LEGATO!

Ties & Slurs

2. Write **TIE** or **SLUR** in the box under each pair of notes, as shown in the first box:

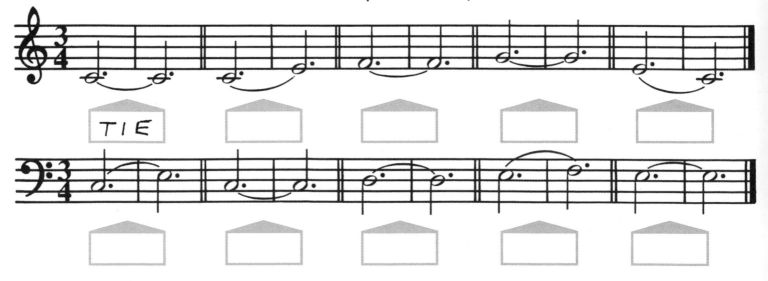

TIE

Measuring 3rds

Assign with Lesson Book p.31

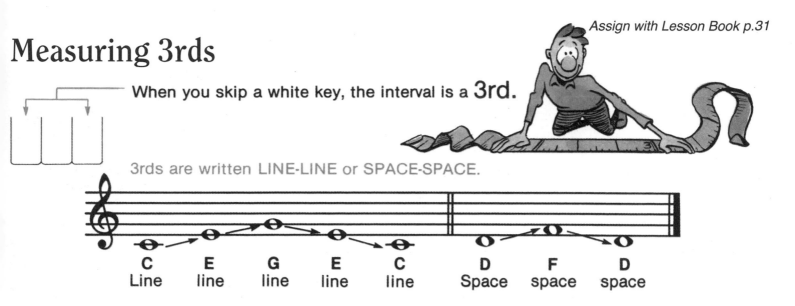

When you skip a white key, the interval is a **3rd.**

3rds are written LINE-LINE or SPACE-SPACE.

C	E	G	E	C	D	F	D
Line	line	line	line	line	Space	space	space

1. Trace the arrows between the notes while saying the words above the notes.

2. Write the note name under each note, then play, saying "Up a 3rd," etc.

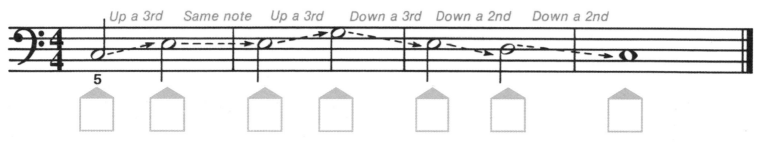

Up a 3rd   Same note   Up a 3rd   Down a 3rd   Down a 2nd   Down a 2nd

3. Write the name of the interval (2nd or 3rd) in the box below each pair of notes, as shown in the first box.

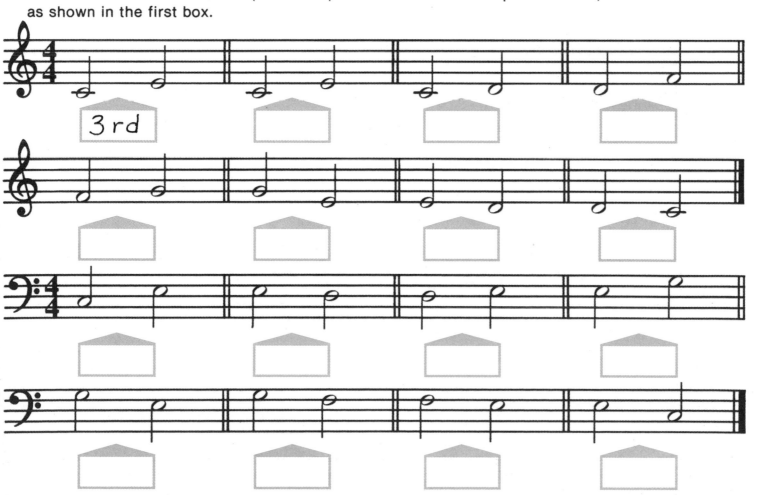

3rd

Assign with Lesson Book p.34

Melodic Intervals

When notes are played separately they make a MELODY.
We call the intervals between melody notes MELODIC INTERVALS.

1. After each note, add another MINIM making a melodic interval
   ABOVE the given note, as indicated.

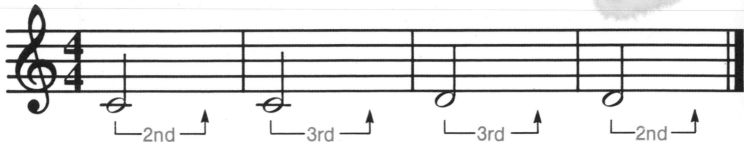

2. After each note, add another MINIM making a melodic interval
   BELOW the given note, as indicated.

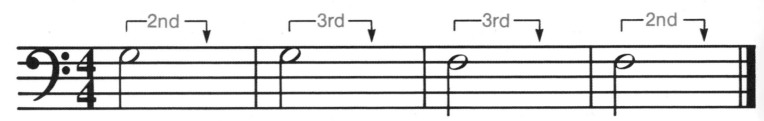

Harmonic Intervals

When notes are played together they make HARMONY.
We call the intervals between these notes HARMONIC INTERVALS.

The notes of **HARMONIC 2nds** are written SIDE-BY-SIDE, touching: The notes of **HARMONIC 3rds** are written ONE ABOVE THE OTHER: 𝄞

3. Above each note, add another SEMIBREVE making a harmonic interval
   ABOVE the given note, as indicated.

        2nd   3rd   3rd   2nd

4. Below each note, add another SEMIBREVE making a harmonic interval
   BELOW the given note, as indicated.

        2nd   3rd   2nd   3rd

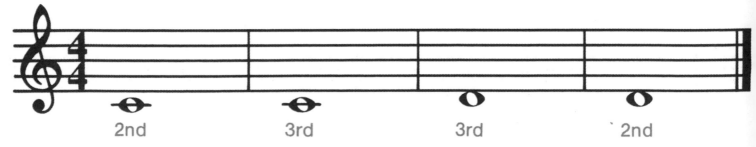

Crotchet Rests

RESTS are signs of SILENCE.

 This is a **CROTCHET REST** or **QUARTER REST**.
It means REST FOR THE VALUE OF A CROTCHET.

COUNT "1" FOR EACH CROTCHET REST!

1. Trace the 2nd crotchet rest, then draw 5 more.

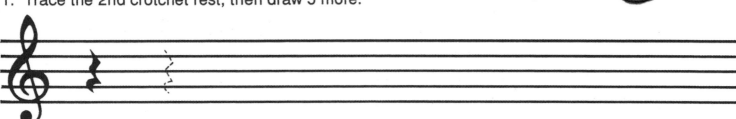

2. Under each note or rest in the following line of music, write the number of counts it receives.
3. Play and count.

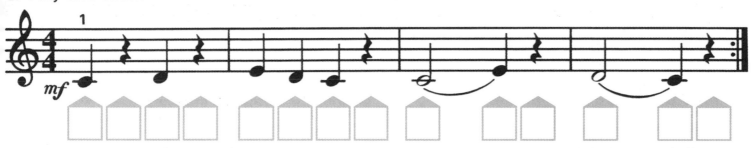

4. Add the values of the notes or rests in each problem and put the total below each line, as shown in the first example.

Fish Talk

Moderately slow

1. When my gold - fish   talks to   me, he   says, "_____."
2. He's as   qui - et   as can be, he   says, "_____."

5. Play FISH TALK and COUNT.

6. Play and sing or say the words. Make a fish face with your mouth for each rest, if you wish.

Measuring 4ths

Assign with Lesson Book p.3

When you skip 2 white keys, the interval is a **4th.**

4ths are written LINE-SPACE or SPACE-LINE.

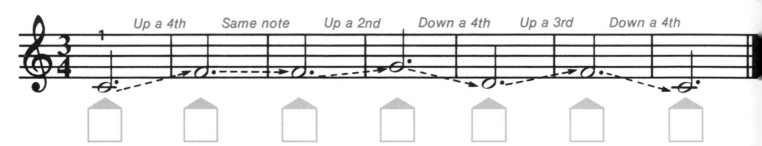

1. Trace the arrows between the notes while saying the words above the notes.
2. Write the name under each note, then play, saying "Up a 4th," etc.

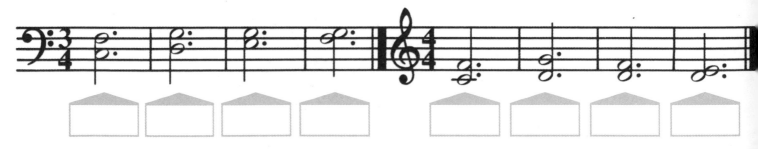

3. The intervals in the next line are _____ (melodic or harmonic) intervals.
4. Write the name of the interval in the box below each pair of notes.

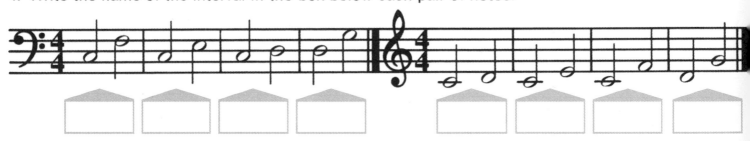

5. The intervals in the next line are _____ (melodic or harmonic) intervals.
6. Write the name of each interval in the box below it.

7. In each bar below, write another note to make the indicated harmonic interval.

Semibreve Rests

▬ This is a **SEMIBREVE OR WHOLE REST.**

It means REST FOR THE VALUE OF A SEMIBREVE
or any WHOLE BAR.

1. Fill in the 2nd SEMIBREVE REST, then draw 5 more.
   The SEMIBREVE REST hangs down from the 4th line of the stave.

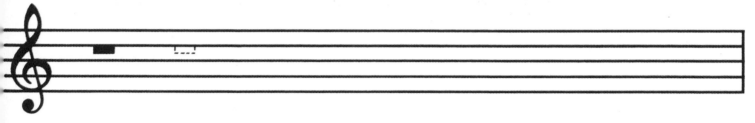

2. In SILENT MARCH and SILENT WALTZ, add a SEMIBREVE REST to each bar that doesn't
   have one.

Silent March

Moderately fast

p

Silent Waltz

Moderately fast

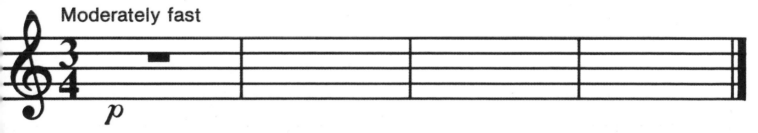

p

3. Play SILENT MARCH with L.H. and count.
4. Play SILENT WALTZ with R.H. and count.

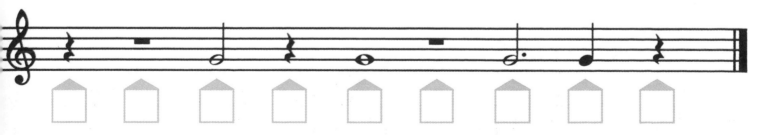

5. Below each rest or note write the number of counts it receives in $\frac{4}{4}$ time.

25

Assign with Lesson Book p.4

Measuring 5ths

When you skip 3 white keys, the interval is a **5th.**

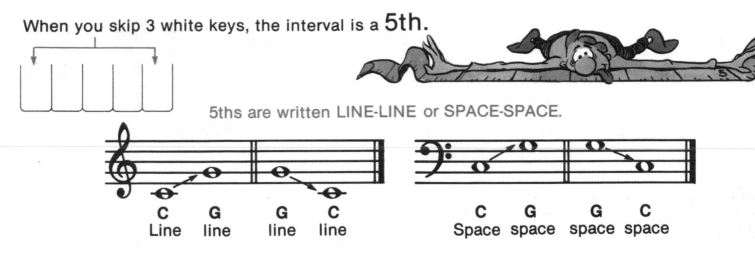

5ths are written LINE-LINE or SPACE-SPACE.

C G G C
Line line line line

C G G C
Space space space space

1. Trace the arrows between the notes while saying the words above the notes.
2. Write the name under each note, then play, saying "Up a 5th," etc.

3. The intervals in the next line are _____ (melodic or harmonic) intervals.
4. Write the name of the interval in the box below each pair of notes.

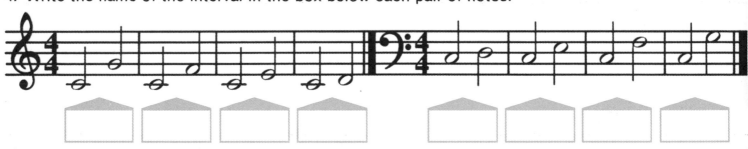

5. The intervals in the next line are _____ (melodic or harmonic) intervals.
6. Write the name of each interval in the box below it.

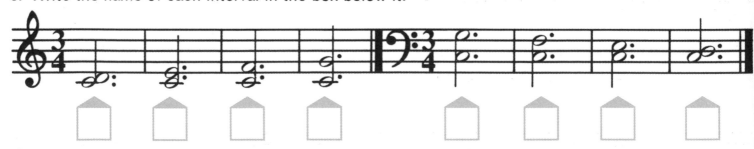

7. In each bar below, add one note to make the indicated harmonic interval.

2nd 3rd 4th 5th 5th 4th 3rd 2nd

G Position

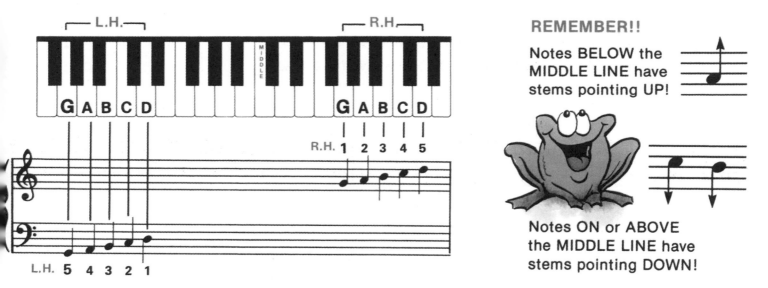

REMEMBER!!

Notes BELOW the MIDDLE LINE have stems pointing UP!

Notes ON or ABOVE the MIDDLE LINE have stems pointing DOWN!

1. Write the L.H. notes in the BASS stave, under the squares. Use CROTCHETS.
   Turn the stems of G A B & C **UP.** Turn the stem of D **DOWN.**

2. Write the R.H. notes in the TREBLE stave, under the squares. Use CROTCHETS.
   Turn the stems of G & A **UP.** Turn the stems of B C & D **DOWN.**

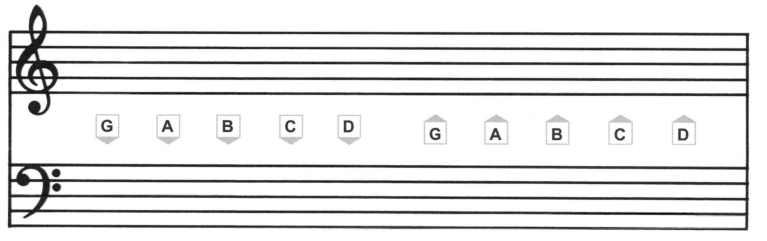

Spelling Game

3. Write the name of each note in the square below it to spell familiar words.

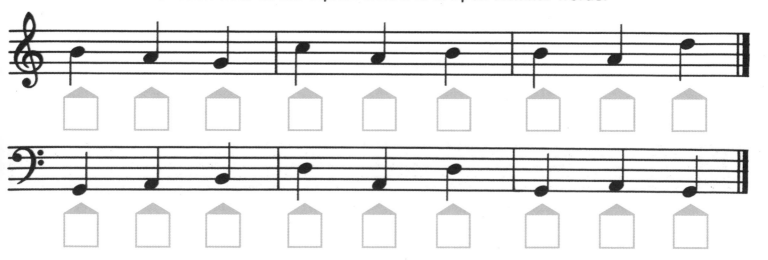

Melodic Intervals in G Position

1. Write the names of the notes in the squares above the staves.
2. Write the names of the intervals in the boxes below the staves.

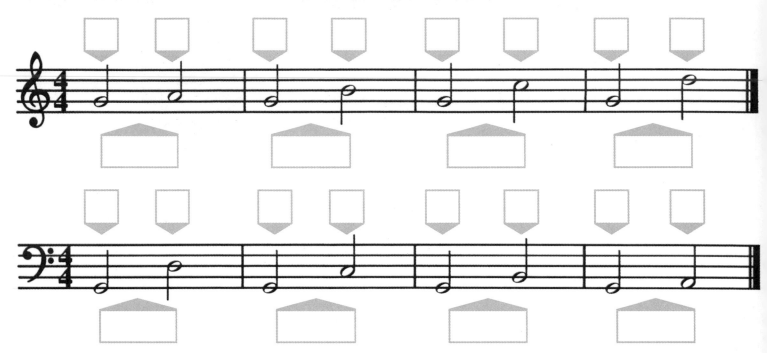

Harmonic Intervals in G Position

3. Write the names of the notes in the squares above the staves. Write the name of the lower note in the lower square, and the name of higher note in the higher square.

4. Write the names of the intervals in the boxes below the staves.

Reviewing Rests

RESTS ARE SIGNS OF SILENCE

CROTCHET REST: means rest for the value of a crotchet.

MINIM REST: means rest for the value of a minim.

SEMIBREVE REST: means rest for the value of a semibreve or for any whole bar.

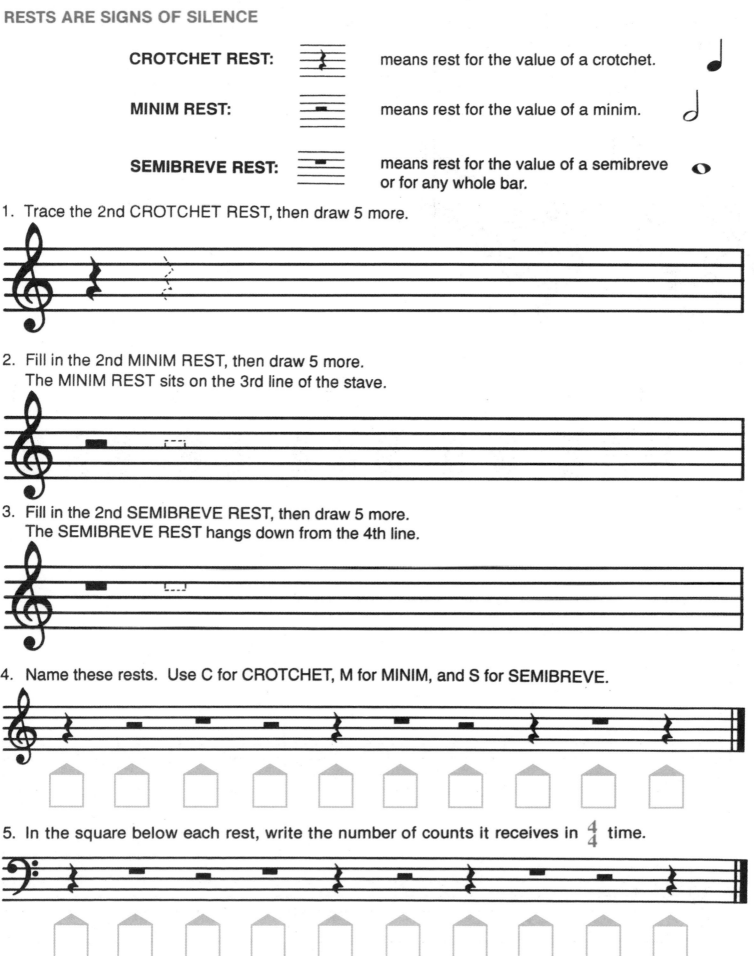

1. Trace the 2nd CROTCHET REST, then draw 5 more.

2. Fill in the 2nd MINIM REST, then draw 5 more.
   The MINIM REST sits on the 3rd line of the stave.

3. Fill in the 2nd SEMIBREVE REST, then draw 5 more.
   The SEMIBREVE REST hangs down from the 4th line.

4. Name these rests. Use C for CROTCHET, M for MINIM, and S for SEMIBREVE.

5. In the square below each rest, write the number of counts it receives in $\frac{4}{4}$ time.

Assign with Lesson Book p.4●

Sharps

The **SHARP SIGN** ♯ before a note means play the next key to the right, whether black or white.

1. Make some SHARP SIGNS:

First, draw the two vertical lines.   Then add the heavy slanting lines.

Draw 4 sharp signs here.

2. Write the names of the ♯ keys in the boxes:

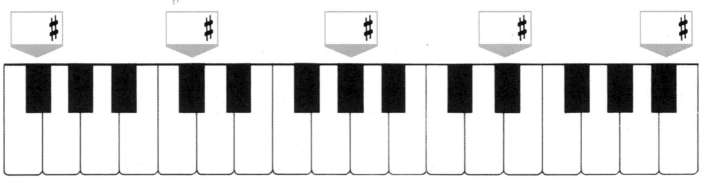

3. Change each of these notes to a sharp note. Play each with R.H. 3 or L.H. 3.

When writing sharp signs, be sure the CENTRE of the sign is on the line or space of the note to be sharpened:

Place the sharp BEFORE the note:

Flats

The **FLAT SIGN** ♭ before a note means play the next key to the left, whether black or white.

1. Make some FLAT SIGNS:

First, draw one vertical line.

Then add the heavier curved line.

Draw 4 flat signs here.

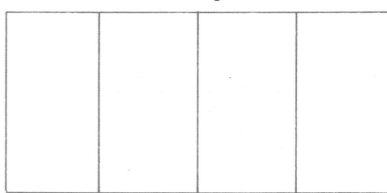

2. Write the names of the ♭ keys in the boxes.

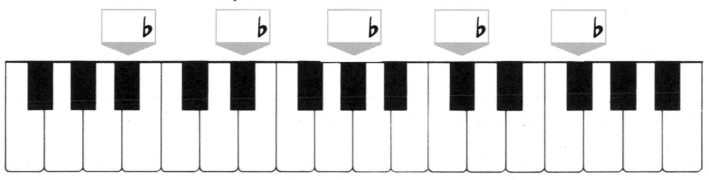

3. Change each of these notes into a flat note. Play each with R.H. 3 or L.H. 3.

Be sure to CENTRE the flat sign on the line or space of the note to be flattened:

Place the flat BEFORE the note: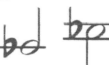

4. Can you read this motto?

ALWAYS  AND YOU'LL NEVER  !

Assign with Lesson Book p.52

Staccato is the Opposite of Legato!

STACCATO notes are SEPARATED or DETACHED.
STACCATO is indicated by a **DOT** over or under a note:

LEGATO notes are SMOOTHLY CONNECTED.
LEGATO is indicated by a **SLUR** over or under a group of notes:

1. Write **S** under each staccato note below.

2. Write **L** under each legato note below.

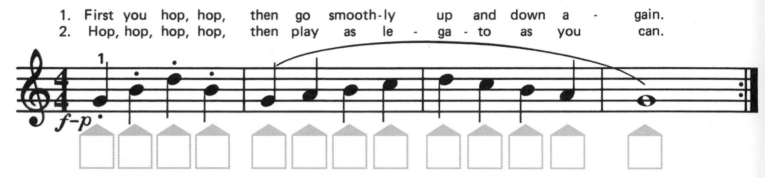

1. First you hop, hop, then go smooth-ly up and down a - gain.
2. Hop, hop, hop, hop, then play as le - ga - to as you can.

3. Play the above. Carefully observe the staccato and legato signs.

Sometimes LEGATO notes are connected smoothly to a STACCATO note. In such a case only the LAST note is played staccato, while the rest are played legato:

L L L S L L L S L S L S L S S S

Indian Voices

4. Write **L** under each legato note.

5. Write **S** under each staccato note.

1. In - dian voi - ces, Hear them ring - ing! Hi - yah, yah, yah! Hi - yah, yah, yah!
2. In - dians danc - ing, In - dians sing - ing! Hi - yah, yah, yah! Hi - yah, yah, yah!

Assign with Lesson Book p.58

Writing Tempo Marks

ALLEGRO   **ANDANTE**   **ADAGIO**

Three Short Pieces

1. Read the words to each of these 3 short pieces, then decide on the best TEMPO marks and DYNAMIC signs and ADD THEM.
2. Add Bar lines.
3. At the end of each, add a sign that means REPEAT.
4. Play the pieces.

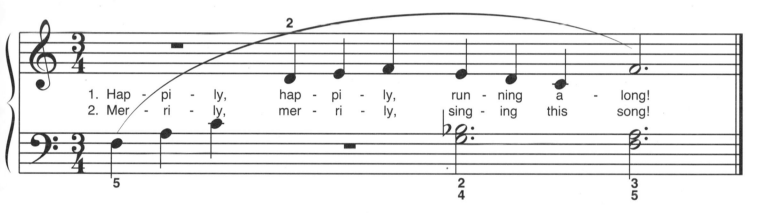

1. Hap - pi - ly, hap - pi - ly, run - ning a - long!
2. Mer - ri - ly, mer - ri - ly, sing - ing this song!

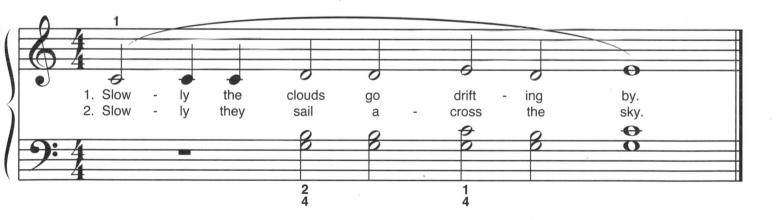

1. Slow - ly the clouds go drift - ing by.
2. Slow - ly they sail a - cross the sky.

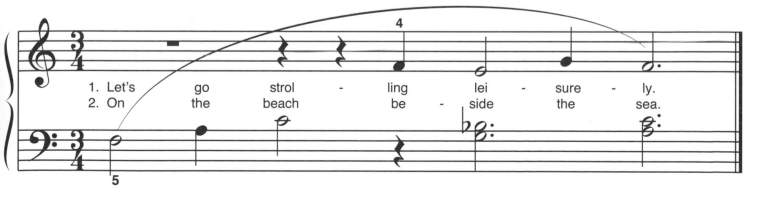

1. Let's go strol - ling lei - sure - ly.
2. On the beach be - side the sea.

Assign with Lesson Book p.5?

Pauses Are to Hold!

A note under a PAUSE ⌒ is held longer than its value.

1. Write the names of the notes in the boxes below.
2. Play. Hold the notes with the pauses longer than their values.
3. Play and say or sing the words.
4. How many pause signs are in this piece? ———

Pauses and Rainbows

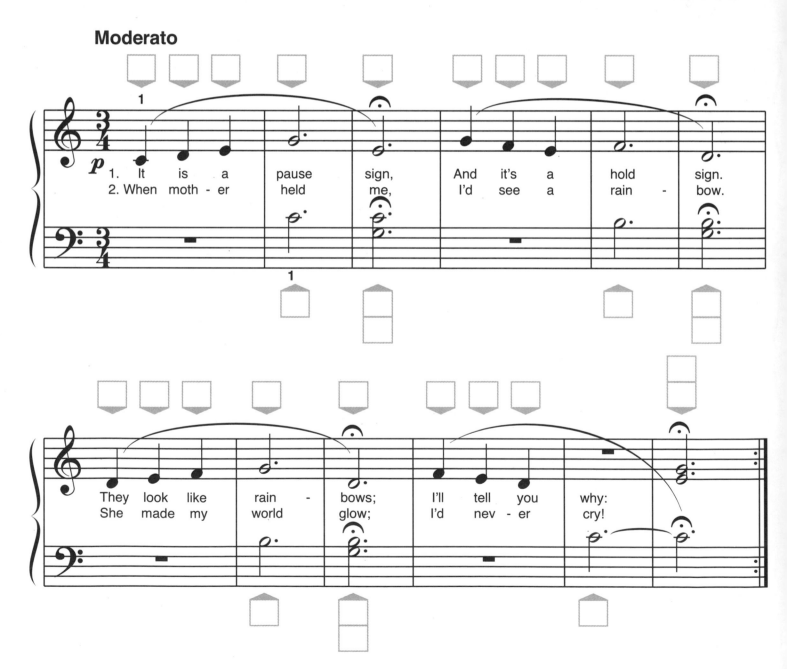

Writing Quavers

Assign with Lesson Book p.61

ONE CROTCHET   **TWO QUAVERS**

QUAVERS are usualled played in PAIRS. They are joined with a BEAM:

1. Change these crotchets to QUAVERS by adding a BEAM to each pair.

> To count music containing quavers, divide each beat into 2 parts:
>
> count: "one-and" or "crotch-et" for each crotchet;
> count: "one-and" or "qua-ver" for each pair of quavers.

2. Play the following while you count aloud: "One-and, one-and," etc.
   Play again, counting "Crotch-et, crotch-et," etc.

Moderato

COUNT: One - and, one - and, one - and,   One -   and,   one - and,   one - and.
or: Crotch - et, crotch - et, crotch - et,   Qua - ver,   qua - ver,   qua - ver.

COUNT: One - and, one - and, one - and,   One -   and,   one - and,   one - and.
or: Crotch - et, crotch - et, crotch - et,   Qua - ver,   qua - ver,   qua - ver.

Assign with Lesson Book p.6

How's Your Italian?

Many Italian terms are used in music in almost every country in the world.
You have learned a lot of them already. Let's see how much Italian you know.

Draw lines connection the dots on the matching boxes.

TEMPO	slow
RITARDANDO	rate of speed
ADAGIO	slowing down
ANDANTE	moderate speed
MODERATO	walking speed
ALLEGRO	from the beginning
Da CAPO	fast
FINE	gradually louder
CRESCENDO	the end
DIMINUENDO	moderately loud
MEZZO FORTE	gradually softer
PIANO	loud
FORTE	soft
LEGATO	detached
STACCATO	return to original speed
A TEMPO	smoothly connected

Assign with Lesson Book p.64

Kookaburra

1. Add bar lines.
2. Play and count.
3. Play and say or sing the words.

Allegro moderato

Remember: In $\frac{2}{4}$ time, a semibreve rest indicates a whole bar of silence.

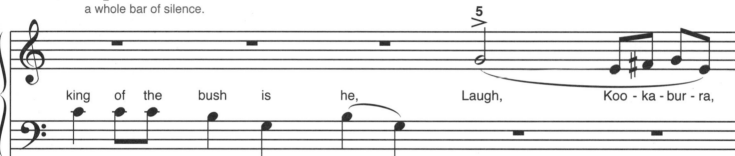

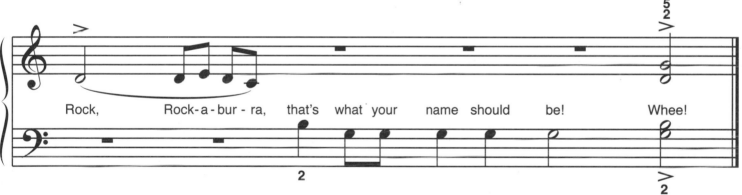

4. In the three lines below, add time signatures at the beginning of each line.
5. Clap (or tap) the rhythm of each line, counting aloud.
6. Say the words of each line in rhythm.

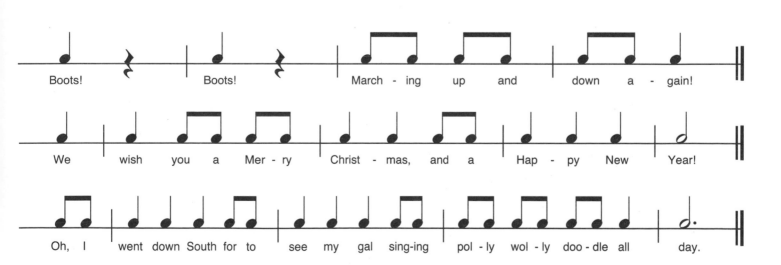

Assign with Lesson Book p.6

Writing G Positions for LH

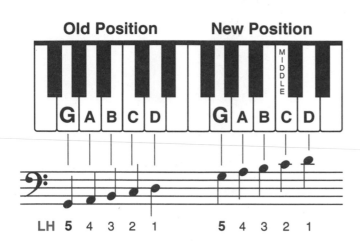

The Big Rock Candy Mountain

1. Write the note names in the boxes ABOVE the notes.
   This will help you learn the new G POSITION.
2. Write the note names in the boxes BELOW the notes.
   This reviews the old G POSITION.
3. Play and count.
4. Play and say or sing the words.

Allegro

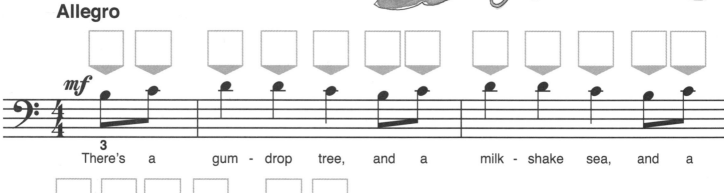

mf

There's a gum - drop tree, and a milk - shake sea, and a

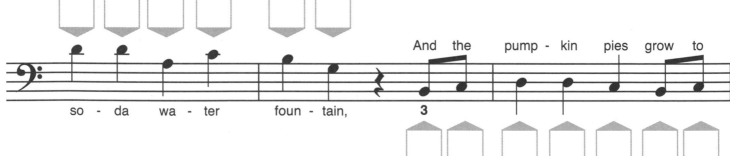

so - da wa - ter foun - tain,

And the pump - kin pies grow to

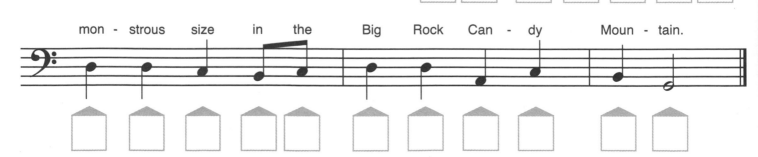

mon - strous size in the Big Rock Can - dy Moun - tain.

The Damper Pedal

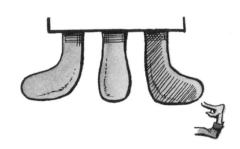

Use the RIGHT FOOT on the RIGHT PEDAL,
called the **DAMPER PEDAL.**

This sign shows when the damper pedal is to be used:

Pedal down   **hold pedal**   **Pedal up**

The music on this page helps you to develop freedom
of movement at the keyboard. The hands play in a new
position in each measure. LH & RH play in either clef.

You will learn how the pedal connects the notes together,
LEGATO, even while the hands are changing positions.

G-B-D-Fs

The first note of each measure is G. The notes in each measure are a 3rd apart.

1. Write the names of the notes in the boxes.
2. Play. (Stems down = LH, stems up = RH.) Hold the pedal down throughout the entire line.

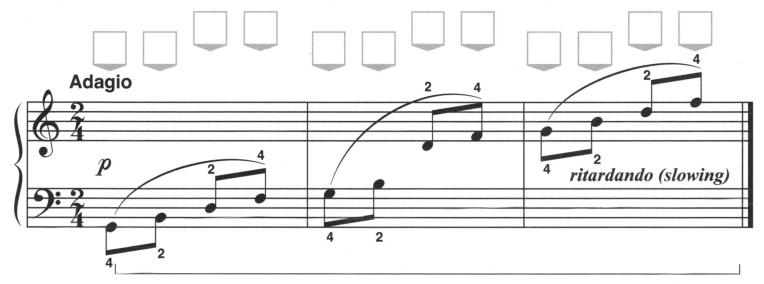

A-C-E-Gs

The first note of each measure is A. The notes in each measure are a 3rd apart.

3. Write the names of the notes in the boxes.
4. Play. (Stems down = LH, stems up = RH.) Hold the pedal down as indicated.

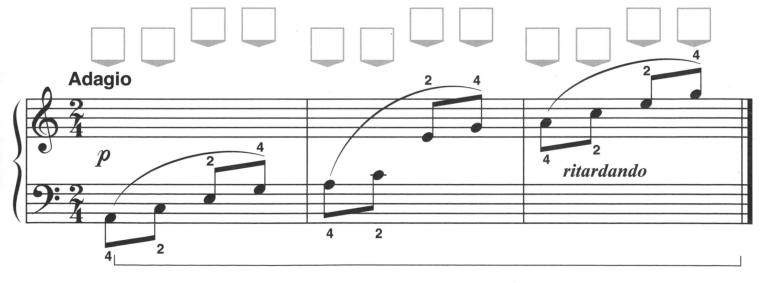

Assign with Lesson Book p.7.

More about Quavers

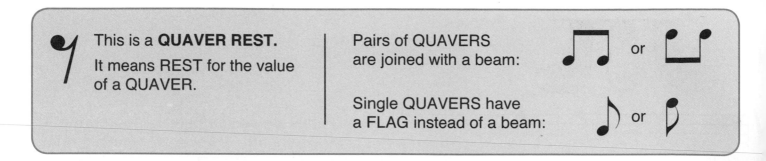

This is a **QUAVER REST.**
It means REST for the value of a QUAVER.

Pairs of QUAVERS are joined with a beam: or

Single QUAVERS have a FLAG instead of a beam: or

1. Make these crotchets into SINGLE QUAVER NOTES.
   Trace the first flag, then add flags to the other notes.

2. Trace the first QUAVER REST, then draw quaver rests between the other notes.

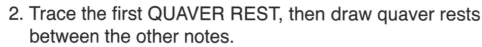

| Quaver | Quaver rest | Quaver | Quaver rest | Quaver | Quaver rest | Quaver | Quaver rest | Quaver |

Reviewing Note & Rest Values

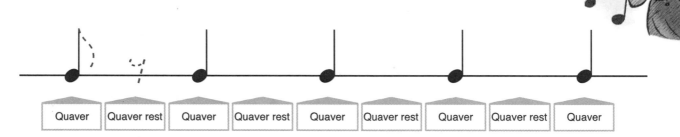

Quaver =   Crotchet =   Minim =   Semibreve = O

Quaver rest =   Crotchet rest =   Minim rest =   Semibreve rest* =
                                     (sits on line)   (hangs down)

***A SEMIBREVE is also used to indicate silence for any WHOLE BAR of** $\frac{2}{4}$, $\frac{3}{4}$ **or** $\frac{4}{4}$ **!**

3. Complete these bars by adding only ONE REST to each bar:

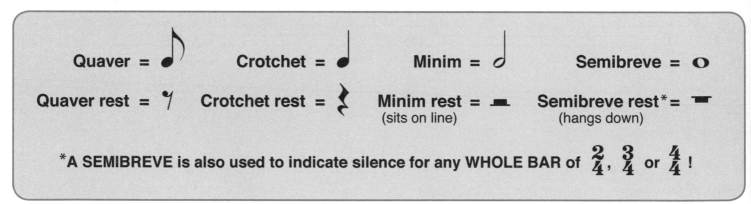

Note Review

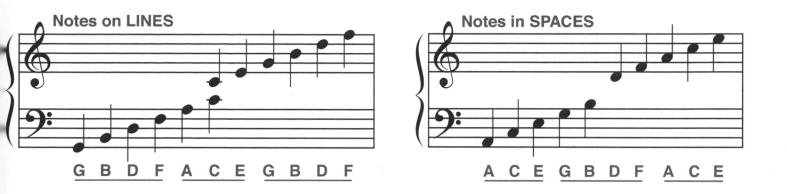

Notes on LINES

G B D F A C E G B D F

Notes in SPACES

A C E G B D F A C E

1. Write the names of the notes in the boxes.
2. Play. Use LH 3 for notes below middle C. Use RH 3 for notes on or above middle C.

Assign with Lesson Book p.7

Theory Review

Intervals

1. Write the number (4th, 5th, etc.) of the melodic interval.

_____   _____   _____   _____

2. Write the number (4th, 5th, etc.) of the harmonic interval.

_____   _____   _____   _____

Sharps and Flats

3. Write higher or lower followed by the name of the second note (see example):